HAPPINESS

summersdale

HAPPINESS

Copyright © Summersdale Publishers Ltd 2013

All rights reserved.

Summersdale Publishers Ltd
46 West Street
Chichester
West Sussex
PO19 1RP
UK

www.summersdale.com

Printed and bound in China

ISBN: 978-1-84953-384-3

Substantial discounts on bulk quantities of Summersdale books are available to corporations, professional associations and other organisations. For details contact Nicky Douglas by telephone: +44 (0) 1243 756902, fax: +44 (0) 1243 786300 or email: nicky@summersdale.com.

To Martha, on your christening

From Philippa + Adam

Introduction

We can travel far and wide to seek happiness, forgetting that happiness is in the journey rather than the destination. This book is filled with quotations to guide and enrich you, along with mindful tips to help reveal your own internal happiness, wherever you are, at any time of day. Enjoy discovering the pleasures of a joyful and more confident approach to life.

Happiness is when what you think, what you say and what you do are in harmony.

Mahatma Gandhi

One joy scatters a hundred griefs.

Chinese proverb

He who sows courtesy
reaps friendship,
and he who plants
kindness gathers love.

St Basil of Caesarea

HAPPINESS IS
NOT SOMETHING
READY MADE.
IT COMES FROM YOUR
OWN ACTIONS.

Dalai Lama

The best way to cheer yourself up is to try to cheer somebody else up.

Mark Twain

Find ecstasy in life;
the mere sense of
living is joy enough.

Emily Dickinson

Exercise! Whether it's a gentle stroll, a toe-tapping dance class or a burst in the gym – the endorphin release will make you smile.

Mindfulness
helps us to regain
the paradise we
thought we had lost.

Thich Nhat Hanh

Happiness is not an
ideal of reason, but
of imagination.

Immanuel Kant

HAVE PATIENCE
AND ENDURE:
THIS UNHAPPINESS
WILL ONE DAY BE
BENEFICIAL.

Ovid

I think I began
learning long ago that
those who are happiest
are those who do the
most for others.

Booker T. Washington

Happiness consists
not in having much,
but in being content
with little.

Marguerite Gardiner

Happiness is the key
to success.

Albert Schweitzer

*Volunteer for
something you care
about like animal
welfare or human
rights – giving is often
more rewarding
than receiving.*

If you want to be
happy, be.

Leo Tolstoy

Independence
is happiness.

Susan B. Anthony

THE RIGHTEOUS MAN IS HAPPY IN THIS WORLD, AND HE IS HAPPY IN THE NEXT.

Siddhārtha Gautama Buddha

Turn your face to the
sun and the shadows
fall behind you.

Maori proverb

Humour is
the great thing, the
saving thing.

Mark Twain

Those who make many friends... make society a better place and lead happy, satisfying lives.

Daisaku Ikeda

*Give away what you
don't need or use.
You'll feel as light
as a feather after
clutter-clearing.*

Our life is what our
thoughts make it.

Marcus Aurelius

He who knows
that enough is
enough will
always have enough.

Lao Tzu

You will never be happier than you expect. To change your happiness, change your expectation.

Bette Davis

THE MOST WASTED
OF ALL DAYS IS
THAT ON WHICH
ONE HAS NOT
LAUGHED.

Nicolas Chamfort

A great obstacle to
happiness is to expect
too much happiness.

Bernard le Bovier de Fontenelle

Most folks are about
as happy as they make
up their minds
to be.

Abraham Lincoln

Call an elderly relative for a chat. Both of you will end up smiling.

Happiness never
decreases by
being shared.

Siddhārtha Gautama Buddha

There are two ways of spreading light: to be the candle or the mirror that reflects it.

Edith Wharton

Happiness... lies in the joy of achievement, in the thrill of creative effort.

Franklin D. Roosevelt

The grand essentials
of happiness are:
something to do,
something to love
and something to
hope for.

Alexander Chalmers

But the man
worthwhile is the one
who will smile when
everything goes
dead wrong.

Ella Wheeler Wilcox

HAPPINESS IS A HABIT – CULTIVATE IT.

Elbert Hubbard

*Wear something
brightly-coloured and
fun – it will keep you
cheerful all day long.*

Happiness is
not a goal; it is a
by-product.

Eleanor Roosevelt

Every lot has enough happiness provided for it.

Fyodor Dostoevsky

Those who bring
sunshine into the lives
of others cannot keep
it from themselves.

J. M. Barrie

We act as though comfort and luxury were the chief requirements of life, when all that we need to make us really happy is something to be enthusiastic about.

Charles Kingsley

So long as we can lose
any happiness,
we possess some.

Booth Tarkington

Happiness is like a butterfly which, when pursued, is always beyond our grasp, but, if you will sit down quietly, may alight upon you.

Nathaniel Hawthorne

*Be generous – give
with grace and
good will.*

A HAPPY LIFE
CONSISTS NOT
IN THE ABSENCE,
BUT IN THE MASTERY
OF HARDSHIPS.

Helen Keller

All the statistics in the
world can't measure
the warmth of a smile.

Chris Hart

Always laugh when you can. It is cheap medicine.

Lord Byron

There is no cosmetic
for beauty like
happiness.

Marguerite Gardiner

Illusory joy is often worth more than genuine sorrow.

René Descartes

Mix a little foolishness with your serious plans. It is lovely to be silly at the right moment.

Horace

*Create small
kindnesses for others
even on the busiest
of days.*

For every minute
you are angry you
lose sixty seconds of
happiness.

Ralph Waldo Emerson

Gladness of heart is
the life of man and the
joyfulness of man is
length of days.

Ecclesiastes

THE ROBBED THAT SMILES, STEALS SOMETHING FROM THE THIEF.

William Shakespeare, *Othello*

He who enjoys doing
and enjoys what he
has done is happy.

Johann Wolfgang von Goethe

Happiness arises in a
state of peace,
not of tumult.

Ann Radcliffe

Grief can take care of itself, but to get the full value of a joy you must have somebody to divide it with.

Mark Twain

*Give compliments
freely – you will make
someone's day!*

If I keep a green
bough in my heart
the singing bird
will come.

Chinese proverb

If only we'd stop trying to be happy we could have a pretty good time.

Edith Wharton

A happy life consists
in tranquillity
of mind.

Marcus Tullius Cicero

A KIND HEART IS A FOUNTAIN OF GLADNESS, MAKING EVERYTHING IN ITS VICINITY FRESHEN INTO SMILES.

Washington Irving

Forget not that the earth delights to feel your bare feet and the winds long to play with your hair.

Kahlil Gibran

Think of all the beauty still left around you and be happy.

Anne Frank

Be warned! A genuine handshake or an affectionate hug can result in a sudden feeling of happiness.

Happiness often
sneaks in through a
door you didn't know
you left open.

John Barrymore

You're the
blacksmith of your
own happiness.

Norwegian proverb

Be glad of life
because it gives you
the chance to love,
to work, to play and
to look up at the
stars.

Henry van Dyke

It is not how much we have, but how much we enjoy, that makes happiness.

Charles Spurgeon

Joy is the will
which labours, which
overcomes obstacles,
which knows triumph.

William Butler Yeats

BE HAPPY.
IT'S ONE WAY OF
BEING WISE.

Colette

Smile at a passer-by –
you'll both feel good.

But what is happiness
except the simple
harmony between
a man and the life
he leads?

Albert Camus

Talk happiness. The world is sad enough without your woe. No path is wholly rough.

Ella Wheeler Wilcox

Pleasure in the task
puts perfection in
the work.

Aristotle

Action may
not always bring
happiness, but there
is no happiness
without action.

Benjamin Disraeli

Every day, tell at least one person something you like, admire or appreciate about them.

Richard Carlson

Greater happiness
comes with simplicity
than with complexity.

Siddhārtha Gautama Buddha

If you're feeling at a low ebb, throw yourself into a job that needs doing and before you know it, you'll be whistling while you work.

IF YOU WANT OTHERS TO BE HAPPY, PRACTISE COMPASSION. IF YOU WANT TO BE HAPPY, PRACTISE COMPASSION.

Dalai Lama

Let us be of good cheer,
remembering that the
misfortunes hardest to
bear are those which
never happen.

James Russell Lowell

One must never
look for happiness:
one meets it by
the way.

Isabelle Eberhardt

To render ourselves
happy is to love our
work and find in it
our pleasure.

Françoise Bertaut de Motteville

There is no duty
which we so much
underrate as the duty
of being happy.

Robert Louis Stevenson

There is only one happiness in life, to love and be loved.

George Sand

AGAINST THE ASSAULT OF LAUGHTER NOTHING CAN STAND.

Mark Twain

Happy times are often ordinary and low key – pottering around in your home or spending relaxing time with your family.

Happiness is the meaning and the purpose of life, the whole aim and end of human existence.

Aristotle

A handful of
happiness is better
than a load full of
wisdom.

Russian proverb

All animals, except man, know that the principal business of life is to enjoy it.

Samuel Butler

True happiness... is not attained through self-gratification, but through fidelity to a worthy purpose.

Helen Keller

HAPPINESS IS
A PERFUME YOU
CANNOT POUR ON
OTHERS WITHOUT
GETTING A FEW DROPS
ON YOURSELF.

Ralph Waldo Emerson

If you're interested in finding out more about our gift books, follow us on Twitter: @Summersdale

www.summersdale.com